I am delighted to have you play football.
I believe in rough, manly sports.

–Theodore Roosevelt

Raspberry Sun Tea

6 raspberry herbal teabags   1/4 c. sugar
3 qts. cold water   Garnish: fresh mint sprigs

Place teabags in a one-gallon glass container, add cold water.
Set the container on your sunny porch, patio or windowsill for
several hours. Remove teabags; add sugar and stir well. Chill.
Pour into tall chilled glasses filled with ice; garnish with mint
sprigs. Makes 3 quarts.

A neighborhood block party is a great way
to celebrate before the "big game."
Make it memorable...top picnic tables with
placemats or table runners cut from
green outdoor carpeting, available at home
improvement stores. Sure to make any
table look like a football field!

Sparkling Punch

8 c. cranberry juice, divided
3 T. sugar
12 whole allspice

3 short cinnamon sticks
3 bottles pink champagne or
   ginger ale, chilled

Combine 2 cups cranberry juice, sugar, allspice and cinnamon in a saucepan over high heat. Reduce heat to low, cover and simmer 10 minutes. Let cool and refrigerate until chilled. In a pitcher or punch bowl, strain cranberry mixture, discarding spices. Add remaining cranberry juice and champagne or ginger ale. Serve at once. Makes 16 cups.

Keep bottles of soda
frosty in a metal pail
sporting hometown
colors...it's easy to make!
Rub the pail with steel wool
and add the team colors
using enamel paint. Let dry
overnight, then top with
acrylic spray sealer.

Fresh Squeezed Lemonade

1 c. sugar
5 c. cold water
juice of 8 lemons

Garnish: mint sprigs or
lemon peel

Combine all ingredients in a large pitcher and chill. Serve in
tall glasses garnished with mint sprigs or lemon peel twist.
Makes 5 cups.

Fruit Smoothie

2 c. milk
1/2 c. orange juice
8-oz. container
    vanilla yogurt

1 banana, sliced
1 c. strawberries, hulled
1 c. crushed ice

Combine all ingredients in a blender; mix until smooth.
Makes 4 servings.

Score a touchdown
with a tailgate decked
out in hometown colors!
Visit a local party supply store for pom-poms,
strings of battery-operated lights and balloons,
then give the kids football whistles and soft
footballs to toss around during halftime.

Spiced Hot Cider

1 gal. cider
1 c. brown sugar, packed
6-oz. can frozen orange juice
   concentrate
1 cinnamon stick
3 whole cloves
3 whole allspice

Heat all ingredients and simmer until heated through and sugar is dissolved. Remove spices before serving. Serves 10.

Minty Hot Chocolate

1 c. powdered milk
1 c. sugar
1/4 c. hot chocolate mix
1/4 c. mint chocolate chips
1/2 c. mini marshmallows

Mix together all ingredients; store in an airtight container. Use 2/3 cup boiling water to 1/3 cup mix. Makes 8 servings.

Any hometown game
can be a celebration!
Make the evening
special...break out
the sparklers!

5

Life-of-the-Party Snack Mix

2 c. bite-size crispy wheat
  cereal squares
2 c. bite-size crispy corn
  cereal squares
2 c. bite-size crispy rice
  cereal squares
3 c. thin pretzel sticks

13-oz. jar mixed nuts
1 t. garlic salt
1/2 t. seasoned salt
2 T. grated Parmesan cheese
1/3 c. butter, melted
1/3 c. Worcestershire sauce

In a large paper bag, mix together cereals, pretzels and nuts
along with garlic salt, seasoned salt and cheese. Empty bag
into a large bowl and sprinkle butter and Worcestershire sauce
over mixture; combine gently with your hands. Pour mixture
into a 4-quart slow cooker and heat on low setting for 3 to
4 hours. Tear open the bag used to originally mix the snack
mix and spread flat on a counter. Spread heated snack mix
onto bag and let dry for one hour, letting the paper absorb
excess moisture. Store in airtight containers. Makes about
10 cups.

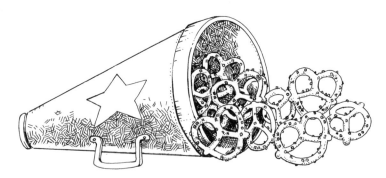

Giant megaphones are great for serving grab & go
snacks like Life-of-the-Party Snack Mix. Just lay them
on the buffet picnic table and fill...a snap!

Home Team Advantage Snack Mix

3 c. popped unsalted popcorn
2 c. mini pretzels
3 c. nacho cheese-flavored
chips
2 4-oz. cans shoestring
potato sticks

1 c. peanuts
1/2 c. margarine, melted
1 T. dried parsley
1/2 t. Italian seasoning
1/2 t. chili powder
1/2 t. garlic powder

In a large bowl, combine the first 5 ingredients. Mix together melted margarine and spices; pour over snack mixture in large bowl. Toss gently until evenly coated. Spread out onto ungreased jelly-roll pan. Bake, uncovered, at 350 degrees for 15 to 20 minutes. Stir twice during baking. Cool, uncovered, and store in airtight containers. Makes about 10 cups.

Scoop Home Team Advantage Snack Mix into a thermos sporting a favorite football team's colors...the thermos will come in handy long after the snack's been enjoyed!

Artichoke Seafood Dip

1 c. mayonnaise
1 c. grated Parmesan cheese
14-oz. can artichoke hearts,
   drained and diced

1/2 c. flaked crabmeat
1 round loaf sourdough
   bread

Combine first 4 ingredients together in a microwave-safe bowl; microwave on high until mixture bubbles. Hollow out round loaf of bread, cubing and reserving removed bread for dipping; pour dip into hollowed-out loaf to serve. Serve warm. Serves 8.

Shape a new deflated basketball, football or soccer ball into a bowl and fill it to the rim with tortilla chips or extra bread cubes for Artichoke Seafood Dip!

Chili-Cheese Dip

8-oz. pkg. cream cheese,
    softened
10-1/2 oz. can chili
    without beans

2 c. shredded Cheddar cheese
Garnish: tortilla chips,
    corn chips

Spread cream cheese in the bottom of an ungreased
13"x9" baking pan; spread chili on top. Sprinkle with cheese.
Bake at 350 degrees for 20 minutes. Serve with tortilla or corn
chips. Serves 10.

Score big with football-shaped
invitations cut from
corrugated cardboard. Jot the
party information on the back.
Then, on the front, punch holes
for football lacing and tie on a
white shoelace. Fun!

9

Chicken Enchilada Dip

3 boneless, skinless
  chicken breasts
8-oz. pkg. cream cheese,
  softened
1-1/3 c. shredded
  Cheddar cheese
1 t. garlic, minced
1-1/2 T. chili powder
1 t. cumin
1 t. dried oregano

1 t. paprika
cayenne pepper to taste
hot pepper sauce to taste
1 bunch fresh cilantro,
  chopped
4 green onions, chopped
10-oz. can diced tomatoes
  with green chiles
tortilla chips

Cover chicken with water in a saucepan. Cook over low heat
for 30 minutes or until juices run clear; let cool. Finely chop
chicken; set aside. In a large mixing bowl, mix cheeses until
creamy and well blended. Add garlic, chili powder, cumin,
oregano, paprika, cayenne pepper and pepper sauce; mix well.
Add chicken, cilantro, green onions and tomatoes. Gently fold
into the cheese mixture. Refrigerate overnight for full flavor.
Serve with tortilla chips. Makes about 6 cups.

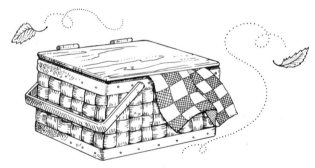

If game night weather turns rainy, it's still easy to have
family tailgating fun...lift up the tailgate, spread a stadium
blanket or checkered tablecloth inside the back and enjoy
pregame munchies, picnic style!

Touchdown Taco Dip

16-oz. can refried beans
8-oz. pkg. cream cheese
1-1/4 oz. pkg. taco
   seasoning mix
1 tomato, chopped

1/4 c. onion, chopped
1/2 c. shredded
   Cheddar cheese
Garnish: sour cream
tortilla chips

Spread refried beans over the bottom of a 9" pie pan; set aside.
Combine cream cheese and taco seasoning; spread over beans.
Sprinkle with tomato, onion and Cheddar cheese; bake at
375 degrees for 25 to 30 minutes. Dollop with sour cream
before serving; serve with tortilla chips. Serves 6.

Tall, skinny terra cotta
pots are ideal for
holding all those long
veggies like carrots,
green onions and celery.
Be sure to pick up new pots,
rinse well and line with
parchment paper before
adding vegetables.

Undefeated Bacon-Cheese Dip

1 lb. bacon, crisply cooked
   and crumbled
2 8-oz. pkgs. shredded
   Cheddar cheese
1/2 c. chopped pecans

2 c. mayonnaise-type salad
   dressing
1 onion, chopped
assorted crackers, celery

Combine bacon, cheese, pecans, salad dressing and onion; mix well. Serve with crackers and celery. Makes about 7 cups.

Keep extra veggie dippers in the refrigerator crisp
by wrapping them in damp paper towels and storing in
a plastic zipping bag. More veggies and Undefeated
Bacon-Cheese Dip, please!

Hot Pepperoni Dip

2 c. shredded mozzarella
  cheese
2 c. shredded sharp Cheddar
  cheese
2 c. mayonnaise
4-oz. can diced green chiles,
  drained

1 red onion, chopped
2 to 3 jalapeño peppers,
  diced
10 to 20 pepperoni slices
baguette slices, assorted
  crackers

Combine cheeses, mayonnaise, chiles, onion and peppers;
place in an ungreased 13"x9" baking pan. Layer pepperoni on
top; bake at 350 degrees for 45 minutes. Serve with baguette
slices and crackers. Serves 10.

Retro tin picnic baskets make great carry-alls for any
gathering. They're roomy enough to keep all the goodies
organized and easily wipe clean with a damp cloth.

Tortilla Roll-Ups

8-oz. pkg. cream cheese,
   softened
1/3 c. salsa
1/4 c. green onion, chopped

1/2 t. garlic powder
1/2 t. chili powder
1/2 t. cumin
12 flour tortillas

Blend cream cheese until light and fluffy; mix in salsa, onion, garlic powder, chili powder and cumin. Spread evenly over tortillas; roll and refrigerate until firm, at least 2 hours. Cut into one-inch slices. Serves 12.

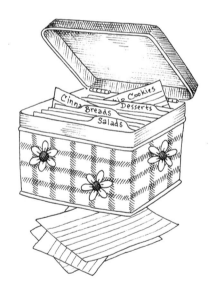

Swap recipes with tailgating neighbors...a terrific way
to try something new!

Party Rye Snack Pizzas

1 lb. ground sausage
16-oz. pkg. pasteurized
    processed cheese spread
2 T. catsup
1/8 t. Worcestershire sauce

1/8 t. dried oregano
1/8 t. garlic salt
2 loaves sliced party
    rye bread

Brown and drain sausage. Add remaining ingredients; blend well. Spread on slices of bread. Place bread on an ungreased baking sheet and bake at 450 degrees for 5 minutes or until bubbly. Serves 6 to 8.

A great gift for Dad! Give a platter of Party Rye Snack Pizzas with a coupon good for an indoor tailgating party...uninterrupted football coverage complete with his favorite snacks and drinks.

Hot Poppers

8-oz. pkg. cream cheese, softened
8-oz. pkg. shredded Cheddar cheese
1/4 c. mayonnaise
15 jalapeños, halved lengthwise and seeded

2 eggs, beaten
1/2 T. milk
1-1/2 c. corn flake cereal, crushed

Combine cheeses and mayonnaise in a medium bowl. Fill jalapeño halves with mixture; set aside. Blend eggs and milk in a small bowl; place cereal in a second small bowl. Dip stuffed jalapeño halves into egg mixture, then roll in cereal to coat. Arrange on a lightly greased baking sheet. Bake at 350 degrees for 30 minutes, or until cheese is golden and bubbly. Makes 2-1/2 dozen.

Pack disposable plates and cups for a game day get-together. Who wants to do the dishes after having so much fun?

Running-Back Stuffed Mushrooms

8-oz. pkg. cream cheese, softened
1 bunch green onions, chopped
8 to 10 slices bacon, crisply cooked and crumbled
10 to 12 mushrooms, stems removed

Mix cream cheese, onions and bacon; spoon mixture into mushroom caps. Arrange on ungreased baking sheets; bake at 300 degrees for 10 to 20 minutes. Makes 10 to 12.

Super Cheese Ball

2 8-oz. containers flavored spreadable cream cheese
1/2 to 1 c. favorite shredded cheese
1/2 to 3/4 c. finely chopped pecans
Optional: hot pepper sauce to taste

Blend cream cheese and shredded cheese in a medium bowl; add pepper sauce, if desired. Form into a ball and roll in chopped pecans; wrap in plastic wrap and refrigerate for an hour before serving. Makes one cheese ball.

For tasty fun at the next tailgate party, turn any favorite cheese ball recipe into a "football." Just shape, sprinkle with paprika and pipe on sour cream or cream cheese "laces"...so easy!

Zucchini Appetizers

3 c. zucchini, thinly sliced
1/2 t. dried oregano
1/2 c. onion, finely chopped
1/2 c. grated Parmesan
   cheese
1 clove garlic, minced
1/2 t. seasoned salt

1 c. biscuit baking mix
1/2 t. salt
1/2 c. oil
4 eggs, slightly beaten
2 T. fresh parsley, chopped
1/8 t. pepper

Mix all ingredients together and spread in a greased
13"x9" pan. Bake at 350 degrees until golden, about
25 minutes. Cut into small squares for appetizers. Serves
8 to 10.

Invite friends over for a cookout before the big game.
Begin with invitations made of felt in the shape of
pennants or use a permanent marker to write party
information on small plastic footballs.

Quarterback-Sneak Squares

8-oz. pkg. cream cheese,
   softened
1/4 c. margarine, melted
1/2 t. salt
1 t. pepper
1/4 c. milk
2 T. green onion, chopped

4 c. cooked chicken,
   shredded
2 8-oz. tubes refrigerated
   crescent rolls
10-3/4 oz. can cream of
   chicken soup
2/3 c. sour cream

Blend cream cheese, margarine, salt, pepper, milk and onion
together; mix in chicken. Set aside. Unroll crescent rolls and
form 8 squares by pinching 2 rolls together; spoon 1/2 cup
chicken mixture onto each square. Fold up each corner; pinch
sides together to form a pocket. Place on an ungreased baking
sheet; bake at 325 degrees for 20 minutes or until golden. Set
aside. Combine soup and sour cream in a sauce pan; heat
through. Pour over squares before serving. Makes 8.

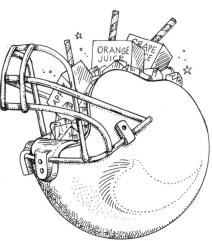

Keep the hometown
game fun for little
ones too...toss
crushed ice and juice
boxes into upside-down
football helmets.

BBQ Slow-Cooker Chicken

4 boneless, skinless chicken
   breasts
3/4 c. chicken broth

1 c. barbecue sauce
1 sweet onion, sliced
salt and pepper to taste

Place all ingredients in a slow cooker; stir gently. Heat on high setting for 3 hours or on low setting for 6 to 7 hours. Makes 4 servings.

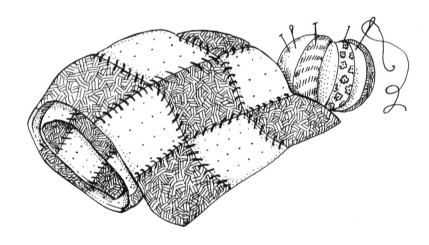

Nighttime football games can be chilly...stitch together a fleece lap blanket in team colors to keep cozy & warm. Fleece doesn't need hemming around the edges, so it couldn't be easier.

Blue-Ribbon Barbecue Ribs

3/4 c. catsup
3/4 c. water
1 c. onion, chopped
2 T. sugar
1 T. Worcestershire sauce

1/4 t. paprika
1/4 t. cayenne
1/4 t. chili powder
2 lbs. pork spareribs

Combine all ingredients except the ribs in a saucepan; bring to a boil. Place ribs in a greased 13"x9" baking pan; pour sauce over ribs. Bake at 375 degrees for 1-1/2 hours. Serves 4.

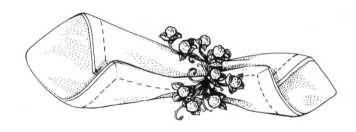

Blue-Ribbon Barbecue Ribs are delicious...and gooey!
If the party is outside, be sure to bring along some
moist towelettes or napkins to clean up little sticky hands
and faces!

Spicy Buffalo Wings

2-1/2 lbs. chicken wings
4-oz. bottle hot pepper sauce

1/2 c. butter, melted
2 T. white vinegar

Arrange chicken in a 13"x9" greased baking pan. Bake at
425 degrees for one hour, turning frequently. Remove from
oven; set aside. Whisk hot sauce, butter, and vinegar together;
pour over chicken. Toss gently to coat. Serves 4 to 6.

Kids don't want to miss all the pre-game fun,
so tote dinner along to enjoy at the stadium.
Turn deflated footballs into serving plates by
filling each with a sandwich, bag of chips and
a couple of cookies...they'll be a hit!

Sesame Chicken Wings

2-1/2 lbs. chicken wings	3 T. soy sauce
1 T. black beans	1-1/2 T. rice wine
1 T. water	1/8 t. pepper
1 T. oil	1 T. sesame seed
2 cloves garlic, pressed	Garnish: green onion, sliced
2 slices fresh ginger, shredded	

Discard chicken wing tips and separate wings into 2 pieces. Mash beans with a ricer or the back of a fork and combine with water; set aside. Add oil to a deep skillet and stir in garlic and ginger; add the chicken wings. Cook over a medium heat, stirring occasionally, until wings are lightly golden. Blend in soy sauce and wine and continue to cook 30 seconds longer. Add black beans and pepper and simmer, covered, 8 to 10 minutes. Uncover skillet and turn temperature to high. Continue to cook, stirring continually until liquid is almost evaporated. Remove skillet from heat; sprinkle on sesame seed, stirring to coat wings. Garnish with green onion before serving. Serves 6.

Make a football-shaped piñata...the kids with love it!

Grilled Brats in Beer

1/2 c. butter
1 onion, thinly sliced and
   separated into rings

12-oz. can beer
16-oz. pkg. bratwurst
5 to 6 hot dog buns

Melt butter in saucepan; add onion and heat until tender. Stir in beer. Heat bratwurst for 20 to 25 minutes on a charcoal grill 3 to 4 inches from coals, turning occasionally, until cooked through. To serve, place in bun and spoon sauce over. Serves 5 to 6.

For small town games, there isn't always lots of room for a big tailgating party, so have a cookout beforehand! Everyone can get in the spirit, enjoy some tasty food and walk to the game together.

Grilled Summer Burgers

1 lb. ground beef	2 t. mustard
1/2 c. onion, chopped	1 t. salt
3 T. catsup	pepper to taste
2 T. green pepper, finely chopped	4 to 5 hamburger buns
1-1/2 T. prepared horseradish	

Combine all ingredients except buns; shape into 4 to 5 patties. Broil in oven or cook on outside grill for 5 minutes. Turn over and broil the other side until done. Place on buns to serve. Makes 4 to 5.

Love to tailgate, but not so wild about the sport? Invite the girls over for a potluck, serve fruity drinks and desserts and watch all the new commercials...sometimes they're the best part of the game!

Monster Cookies

4 c. sugar
2 16-oz. pkgs. brown sugar
16-oz. pkg. margarine
12 eggs
3 16-oz. jars creamy peanut butter
4 t. vanilla extract
2 T. plus 2 t. baking soda

18 c. quick-cooking oats uncooked
16-oz. pkg. semi-sweet chocolate chips
16-oz. pkg. candy-coated chocolates
16-oz. pkg. chopped nuts

Blend together the sugars, margarine, eggs and peanut butter until creamy in a large mixing bowl; stir in baking soda and vanilla. Add remaining ingredients and mix well. Spoon onto greased baking sheets and bake at 350 degrees for 10 to 15 minutes. Makes 18 dozen.

Let guests know where the party is! Fly a team banner from the car antenna or porch.

No-Bake Cookies

1 c. sugar
2 T. baking cocoa
1/4 c. margarine
1/4 c. milk

1/2 t. vanilla extract
1/4 c. creamy peanut butter
1-3/4 c. quick-cooking oats,
uncooked

In a large saucepan over medium heat, combine sugar, cocoa, margarine and milk; stir constantly until sugar is melted. Remove from heat and add vanilla and peanut butter; stir until peanut butter is melted. Add oats; mix until well-combined. Drop by tablespoonfuls onto wax paper and cool in refrigerator. Makes 2 dozen.

Goodies like No-Bake Cookies are safe to set out for the whole game, but make sure desserts with cream cheese frostings, dips and meat dishes are safely presented on the buffet in proper hot or cool containers, depending on the item.

Seven Layer Bars

1/2 c. butter, melted
1-1/4 c. graham cracker
    crumbs
1 c. flaked coconut
6-oz. pkg. semi-sweet
    chocolate chips

1/2 c. butterscotch chips
1 c. chopped nuts
14-oz. can sweetened
    condensed milk

Combine butter and graham cracker crumbs; spread mixture in
a 13"x9" baking pan. Layer remaining ingredients in the order
listed; press down firmly with a spoon. Bake at 350 degrees for
25 to 30 minutes. Cool for 15 minutes before cutting into bars.
Makes 1-1/2 to 2 dozen.

Extras? Not likely, but be sure
to keep some disposable containers on hand
just in case there are leftovers...send some
Seven Layer Bars home with each guest!

Buckeye Bars

1/2 c. butter
1-1/2 c. graham cracker
   crumbs
14-oz. can sweetened
   condensed milk

12-oz. pkg. semi-sweet
   chocolate chips
10-oz. pkg. peanut butter
   chips

Melt butter in a 13"x9" glass baking dish. Spread graham
cracker crumbs over butter. Pour sweetened condensed milk
over crumbs; top with chocolate and peanut butter chips. Press
down firmly with a spoon. Bake at 325 degrees for 25 to
30 minutes. Let cool for 15 minutes before cutting into bars.
Makes 1-1/2 to 2 dozen.

Show your
spirit...dress up a
garden scarecrow in
a hometown football
jersey. Go Team!

TIME TO PARTY!

Keep these simple end goals in mind for a great tailgating party!

10 20 30 40 50

☆ No one wants to miss a minute of the action! Set coolers of frosty beverages near the festivities.

☆ The National Anthem, the marching band, the coin-toss...prepare food ahead of time so you can enjoy pre-game with guests!

☆ Fans big & small come for more than the game! Keep playing cards, face paint and puzzles handy for all those time-outs.

☆ Comfort is key during all 4 quarters. Whether at the stadium or in the living room, provide cushions and blankets...we're here for the long haul and in it to win it!

☆ Decorations put everyone in the winning spirit. Label the house as if you're really there...point guests to the Locker Room to hang their coats, the Concession Stand for appetizers and the Box Seats in front of the TV. The crowd goes wild!

GO GO GO! Extra fun activities...

☆ Take pictures of guests in their team gear!

☆ Play flag football during half-time!

☆ Place bets on who can eat the most wings!

TRY MAKING These Cute Frosted cut-out Cookies!

Football!

Copy and cut out these stencils & use them as a guide for cutting cookies.

Add food coloring to a tube of refrigerated sugar cookie dough to match your favorite team colors. You'll have spirited cookies in no time!

Megaphone!

#1

GO TEAM

SCORE!

Copy, cut out & color this invitation to invite your whole roster over for the biggest and best tailgating party of the season!

INDEX